17

THE
PURR-FECT
CAT BOOK

THE PURR-FECT CAT BOOK

Isha Mellor

PIATKUS

Copyright © 1985 Judy Piatkus (Publishers) Ltd

First published in Great Britain by
Judy Piatkus (Publishers) Ltd, London

British Library Cataloguing in Publication Data

Mellor, Isha
The purr-fect cat book
1. Cats
I. Title
636.8   SF442

ISBN 0-86188-366-7

Edited by Helen Pizzey
Designed by Ken Leeder
Illustrated by Linda Broad
Jacket illustration by Hanife Hassan

Typeset by Phoenix Photosetting, Chatham
Printed and bound by
The Bath Press, Avon

CONTENTS

'A little lion, soft and dainty sweet.'

Graham R Tomson

CATS THROUGH THE AGES

Brief History Of The Domestic Cat

The cat family evolved eight to ten million years ago, before man and before the dog. Our present domestic cat comes from the variety known as *Felis catus*, although the very first species was probably an animal that palaeontologists called *Miacis*, and which was the common ancestor of the big cats – lion, tiger, leopard, jaguar, cheetah, lynx, bobcat, puma and ocelot. The various breeds of domestic cats which we know today were created entirely by man's intervention; they would never have evolved without his influence.

The earliest painting of a cat dates back to about 2600 BC and was found in an Egyptian tomb. The Egyptians revered cats although they did not believe them to be gods, only that gods could use their form. They called the cat *Mau*, a name based on the tone of its voice. The goddess Bast, or Pasht (from which the name 'Puss' may be derived), came to be represented with the head of a cat. To kill or eat the animal was punishable by death, and temple cats, live represen-

tations of Bast, lived in luxury, carefully tended by priests. Temple cats, and even domestic ones, were always mummified and buried with pomp in elaborate coffins and mummy cases. At Beni Hassan, archaeologists discovered three hundred thousand embalmed cats in rows in subterranean tombs. Sometimes mummified mice were laid alongside the cats to provide sustenance in the life hereafter! When the household cat died, members of the family were required by law to shave their eyebrows as a sign of mourning.

The Greeks, however, do not seem to have favoured cats, and scorned the Egyptians who worshipped them. The Persians also took advantage of the nation's reverence of the animal when, in an attack on Egypt, they cunningly advanced carrying cats in their arms so that there would be no danger of retaliation, lest the sacred animals be injured or killed.

It is commonly believed that the Phoenicians brought the first cat to European shores in the second millennium, carrying smuggled Egyptian cats aboard their trading vessels bound for foreign ports. Smuggling cats abroad was a lucrative business which developed as a result of there being a law in Egypt prohibiting the export of the highly-prized animal. In the same way, the domestic cat was introduced to the Eastern parts of the world, but it is thought that there were no cats in China until about 1000 BC. Cats were known to be domesticated at about the same time in India, and occasional references to them have been found in Indian Sanskrit writings. They were used to protect stores of grain.

Those who believed that the Phoenicians actually came to these shores think that domestic cats were possibly introduced into Britain when they visited the Cornish tin mines in 200–100 BC, although many authorities – including St George Mivart, whose book *The Cat* was published in 1881 – believe that no tame cats existed here before the arrival of Julius Caesar. The remains of a cat were found in a Roman Villa at Lullingstone in Kent.

Cats in early Britain were highly esteemed. In the ninth century, for example, a South Wales prince, Hywel Dda, passed laws giving relative values of a cat in money and grain terms, according to its age and usefulness. Penalties also existed at that time for the killing of cats. However, the favour of the animal sadly diminished until, in the Middle Ages, Christians actively persecuted cats on account of the belief that they were associated with witches and acted as their familiars.

Later, at the coronation of Elizabeth I, there is a horrifying account of live cats being caged within an effigy of the Pope to represent the devils which Protestants believed controlled him. After a procession, both the effigy and the cats were burned on a pyre. This feeling against cats was held to be responsible for the spread of the plague in 1664 because there were insufficient numbers to control the rat population.

CATLORE
FOLKLORE

Two animals came out of the Ark who didn't enter it – the pig and the cat. The story goes that when the vessel became overwhelmingly smelly, the inhabitants complained to Noah who then drew his hand along the back of the elephant, bringing forth a pig to eat the filth. The next complaint concerned the rats and mice who were eating all the food. Noah passed his hand along the back of the lion and, when it sneezed, a cat leapt out of its nose! This cat proceeded to gobble up all the vermin – the very first ship's cat.

An Indian legend tells of the time when a cat lived with a tiger. One day, the tiger fell ill and lay shivering with cold. He needed fire, but only man had fire. The cat went to a house to steal some from the hearth, but at the same time found some appetising fish and rice in a bowl. Having devoured this, it was settling down for an after-dinner nap in the warm when it recalled the purpose for which it had come. It took a burning piece of wood from the fire and scampered back to the sick tiger. But, after lighting a comforting blaze for him, the cat announced that it was going to live with man where there was food and warmth and a good new way of life.

A dog and a cat, according to a Russian legend, were put on duty to guard the gates of Paradise. The Devil disguised himself as a mouse and tried to slip through. The dog let it pass, but the clever cat jumped on it and killed it.

A Siamese cat's hooked tail is a reminder of the occasion when an Eastern princess went bathing and gave her jewelled rings to a cat for safe-keeping. The cat instinctively hooked the tip of its tail to prevent the rings threaded on to it from falling off.

Mohammed was a lover of cats, and there is a story that one day, when he found a cat fast asleep on a corner of his robe, rather than disturb the creature from its slumbers he cut the cloth around it instead. It is also said that as a mark of his admiration tabby cats carry the initial M on their foreheads.

In Britain in the Middle Ages, witches, who were considered to be in league with the Devil, were thought to be able to take on animal form. It was also believed that a witch would keep close to her 'familiar' that was a lesser manifestation of the Evil One himself. It therefore became easy to accuse any old and solitary woman of being a witch if she had a pet cat as a companion.

CAT CURES

The gourmet Parson Woodforde of Norfolk has an entry in his famous diary dated 11th March 1791 concerning a stye on his eye:

> 'The Stiony on my right Eye-lid still swelled and inflamed very much. As it is commonly said that the Eye-lid being rubbed by the tail of a black Cat would do it much good if not entirely cure it, and having a black Cat, a little before dinner I made a trial of it, and very soon after dinner I found my Eye-lid much abated of the swelling and almost free from Pain.'

A medieval cure for a fishbone stuck in the mouth or throat was to rub the outside of the spot with some cat dung, after which the bone was said to dislodge itself.

An ointment made with cat dung, mustard seed, onion juice and bear's grease was once a prescription for preventing loss of hair and baldness.

CATS AND RELIGION

We know of the Egyptians' worship of the cat in connection with the goddess Bast. The Romans also allowed cats into their temples, and Muslims let them into the mosques because of the Prophet's love for the animal.

In Britain, cats were not encouraged in church but they often appear in carvings on pew ends, sometimes with mice in their mouths. In a church at Upper Sheringham in Norfolk, a mother cat is portrayed with a kitten held in her jaws. Such homely touches are attributed to an intention to appeal to humble folk as well as to scare away the church mice!

Lewis Carroll is supposed to have found the idea for his grinning Cheshire Cat from observing the face of a cat on a church pillar in a place called Pot Shrigley, Cheshire.

A bitter fight is immortalised on the tomb of Sir Percival Cresacre in Barnburgh Church in Yorkshire, where one may see a wild cat crouching at the knight's feet. Death came to both the man and the cat after they had battled with each other for over three miles before collapsing in the church porch.

The English Nuns' Rule of 1205 stated: 'Dear Sisters, you must keep no beast other than a cat.' This must have been on account of the peaceful and quiet characteristics of the animal.

> For I will consider my Cat Jeoffrey,
> For he is the servant of the Living God,
> duly and daily serving him.

> Christopher Smart (1722–1771)

CATS AND KINGS

'Pussy cat, Pussy cat, where have you been?
I've been up to London to look at the queen.
Pussy cat, Pussy cat, what did you there?
I frightened a little mouse under her chair.'

This rhyme is said to refer to the many democratic entertainments and society tea parties given by Queen Caroline, wife of George IV.

The origin of the phrase 'A cat may look at a king' is attributed to Emperor Maximilian I (1459–1519), who noticed that while he was in conversation with a wood carver, the man's cat was regarding him with a look of deep suspicion. He graciously excused the cat with the words that have subsequently passed into our own language.

When in the 15th century, Sir Henry Wyatt of Allington Castle in Kent, was imprisoned in the Tower of London, his jailer was commanded to provide him with only the basest of nourishment. One day, however, a cat came in through the window and Sir Henry gave it much loving attention. After this the cat would bring in dead pigeons which the jailer was easily persuaded to cook for him as he himself had not provided the food. The prisoner's health was thus preserved; and from the happy day of his release he was seldom seen without a cat at his side.

It is said of Cardinal Wolsey (1475–1530) that, while lovingly stroking the back of his cat with one hand, he would calmly sign a death warrant with the other.

CATS IN SOCIETY

CATS AND PEOPLE

Stately, kindly, lordly friend, Condescend
Here to sit by me.

To A Cat, Algernon Charles Swinburne (1837–1909)

It is said that man likes flattery, with the result that there are more dog lovers than cat lovers. It is true that cats are renowned for their independence of spirit, and give an impression of condescension, even of criticism, when they accept affection and hospitality from humans. The smallest mark of gratitude on the part of the cat is therefore a most precious reward as a cat's grace and favour is bestowed rather than earned.

A man who may be a terror to his employees and a martinet where his wife and children are concerned will often display towards a cat the most remarkable affection and tenderness. (What must his fellow beings feel as they watch the large hand stroking the soft fur, listen to the gentle endearments emanating from the stern lips, and note the smile that emerges when the cat responds playfully?)

But why is it that a cat will make for the one person in the room who will positively shudder at such attention? And why will it totally ignore someone whose one wish is to pet and caress it? Is it an inability to read reactions correctly? One theory is that cats see things on a different plane, where antipathy is seen as sympathy, and vice versa.

A former Minister of Agriculture, whilst trying to push an unpopular pig policy through the Commons stated: 'Cats look down on us, dogs look up to us, pigs is equal.' One can, at least, accept the first two points as true!

'When I play with my cat, who knows whether she is not amusing herself with me more than I with her.'
Michel de Montaigne (1533–92)

CATS OF OFFICE

There are instances where cats have been put on the pay roll of institutions; that is to say they are expected to catch mice in return for the food and shelter offered. Offices, warehouses, barracks, granaries, museums and post offices are among the 'employers' of cats.

Home Office cats are always called Peter, and have been employed since 1883. In 1964, however, a Manx cat appeared on the scene, turned out to be female and had to be named Peta.

Early this century the Reading Room of the British Museum had a cat called Black Jack, who greatly enjoyed the bookish atmosphere and would sit upright on one of the reading desks, calling upon the services of those present whenever he wished to have the door opened for him. One day this system failed and he was imprisoned in a room where newspapers were kept. As a demonstration of his annoyance he sharpened his claws on the bindings. Officialdom decreed that he should be 'fired'. He was reported 'missing, presumed dead', but actually found protection among some museum employees and, after a discreet interval, returned to his post as Reading Room Cat.

With a thought for the future, Black Jack one day brought in a stray kitten, which he aptly presented to the keeper of Egyptian mummified cats. This kitten was named Mike and chose to establish himself at the gatekeeper's lodge, where he carefully checked all who entered or left. He occupied this post from 1909 to 1929, and some lines in his obituary ran:

> 'I scorned the public as it came and went,
> To blandishments and fish indifferent,
> But sat for nineteen years and kept the gate,
> In every hair an Officer of State.'

Much earlier official cats were the ones the Chinese kept near mulberry trees in order to keep rodents away from the silkworms. This custom became so popular that there were eventually not enough to go round and pictures and carvings of cats had to be used as deterrents to augment the live ones.

Apart from those cats who are, or have been, *actively* employed, there was at least one other who earnt his keep without having to twitch a whisker! This was Tiddles, undoubtedly one of the largest domestic cats to survive eleven years weighing an enormous 32 lbs. His home was the ladies lavatory at Paddington Station, London, where he did much to increase the sum earned by the attendants in tips! He went to his permanent heavenly resting place in 1983.

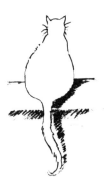

Seen outside a factory gate:
'Required – A cat for light *mouse*work.'

CATS OF MERIT

A medal known as the 'Animal VC' was the Dickin Medal insti-
tuted by Mrs Maria Dickin, the founder of the People's
Dispensary for Sick Animals. During the last war it was
awarded to any animal displaying conspicuous gallantry and
devotion to duty while regularly or temporarily under the
orders, direction or supervision of the Naval, Military or Air
Forces of the Crown, or while attached to the Civil Defence
Force. Of the fifty-three Dickin Medals awarded, eighteen
were presented to dogs, three to horses, thirty-one to
pigeons, and one to a cat. This cat was Simon, who 'served
on HMS *Amethyst* during the Yangtse incident (November
1942–June 1943), disposing of many rats though wounded
by shell blast. Throughout the incident his behaviour was of
the highest order, although a blast was capable of making a
hole in a steel plate of over a foot in diameter.'

Another brave war veteran was Mourka, a Russian cat who
went unchecked through the ruined streets of Stalingrad
during the time of the German siege, carrying despatches
about gun emplacements between groups of undercover
Russians. Messages were strapped invisibly to his body and
it was never suspected that his mission in life was anything
other than self-preservation and scavenging for food.

CAT SUPERSTITION
LONGEVITY

Cats have nine lives; onions and women seven skins.
Proverb

It is not absolutely clear why a cat is said to have nine lives, but the idea seems to come from man's observance of the animal as it goes through life with never a semblance of haste, savouring the long hours of watching and waiting, enjoying the comforts afforded by warmth and acceptable food, and sleeping in all the best places and on the most comfortable laps. It is also clear that a cat makes remarkable escapes from situations of danger. A cat is wise and accepts the gentle passage of time; with nine lives to live, what would be the sense in rushing through just one?

Three tabbies took out their cats to tea,
As well-behaved tabbies as well could be:
Each sat in the chair that each preferred,
They mewed for their milk, and they sipped and purred.
Now tell me this (as these cats you've seen them) –
How many lives had these cats between them?

Three Tabbies, Kate Greenaway (1846–1901)

GOOD AND BAD SIGNS

In Britain it is considered a portent of good luck when a black cat crosses one's path, but in most other European countries, and in the United States, a directly opposite belief is held and a white cat is considered to be the lucky symbol.

It is unlucky to let a cat die in the house, and a cat should never be carried indoors but allowed to enter by itself. However, a three-colour cat will keep a house from catching fire.

Kittens born in May bring ill luck, and it is not a good thing to be photographed with a cat.

To dream of a cat is not a happy omen, indicating as it does that treachery and deceit may be about to befall the dreamer.

When someone in the family has a fever, he should be washed and the water used then thrown over a cat before chasing it outside. The cat will take the fever with it.

Kicking a cat will bring on rheumatism.

If a bachelor accidentally steps on a cat's tail, he will marry before the year is out.

It is a good omen when a cat sneezes near a bride on her wedding morning.

The warning that a cat's breath is poisonous to a human baby is a superstition presumably popularised to alert people to the danger that a sleeping child could be smothered if the animal settles too close to it for warmth.

However, it is also now known that cats can pass on to human babies certain viral infections, transmitted through their breath. They should therefore be kept at a distance because of this.

Chinese parents used to embroider a cat's head on the shoes of a baby learning to walk, to make it surefooted.

When a cat sneezes it is a sign of rain, but if it does so three times there will soon be a cold in the family.

If when washing itself a cat passes a paw behind an ear three times, this is a sign of rain on the way.

SEAFARING CATS

Cats have long been established crew members on board ship as it is thought that they help to maintain good morale, as well as keep the rats under control. Sailors believe that when the ship's cat starts to rush about playfully it is a sign of an oncoming storm. They say that 'the cat has a gale of wind in her tail.' Japanese sailors used to like tortoiseshell cats because they believed them able to banish storm devils.
The sixteenth-century Genoese admiral, Giovanni Andrea Doria, had an enormous pet tabby which he took on all his voyages. Whenever Sir Winston Churchill boarded a vessel, he always asked to be introduced to the ship's cat.

'A cat will never drowne if she sees the shore'
Francis Bacon in 1594

PUB CATS

Hey diddle diddle
The cat and the fiddle.
The cow jumped over the moon
The little dog laughed
To see such craft
While the dish ran after the spoon.

The Cat and the Fiddle is a popular name for a pub and there is much speculation as to its origin. Some attribute it to a corruption of *Le Chat Fidèle*, the faithful cat. Others prefer *Caton le Fidèle*, Caton being a leader of Huguenot silk weavers who came to Congleton in Cheshire during the reign of Elizabeth I and were given rights on the moorland. A *Cat and Fiddle Inn* stands there now.

CAT CHAT

Cats Cradle

Game played with string and fingers. A corruption of *cratch cradle*, cratch being a version of crèche, a manger or crib.

Cat Washing Dishes

Sunlight reflected on ceiling or walls from a bowl of water.

Cat O'Nine Tails

A lash with nine thongs.

Catspaw

Someone who becomes the tool of another. Based on a fable in which the monkey makes the cat flick chestnuts from the fire with its paw.

Cat's Head

Knuckle end of leg of mutton, or a kind of apple.

Cat's Tail

A type of grass.

Cat-call

Whistle used by audiences to express impatience.

Catgut

Not the gut of cats used for stringed instruments but a contracted form of *cattlegut*, which *was* the material used.

Catwalk

Protruding platform on which models walk to display clothes. Possibly so named because of the way models walk with feet placed along one line.

Cat And Dog Life

To be constantly bickering.

To Nurse The Cat	To be idle.
To Shoot The Cat	To vomit after too much drink.
No Room To Swing A Cat	An allusion to the barbaric sport in which a cat was put in a bag and hung from a tree as a target for marksmen. Sometimes two cats were tied by the tails and swung over a rope.
To Bell The Cat	To risk one's life for another. From the fable of the mouse who advised hanging a bell from the cat's neck to warn of her approach; the mouse was not prepared to undertake this dangerous task itself but got others to do so instead.
To Turn The Cat In The Pan	To change sides with dexterity.
Enough To Make A Cat Laugh	i.e. even those least inclined to.
Catwitted	Small-minded, conceited and spiteful.
Cat's Pyjamas/ Whiskers	Anything very good.
Cats	Jazz musicians.
To Rain Cats And Dogs	To rain heavily. Origin obscure but probably a corruption of *catedupe*, which means a waterfall.

CATS IN LITERATURE
AND THE ARTS

LITERARY CATS

Dante had a cat who would helpfully hold a lighted candle between its paws while the poet worked.

Dr Johnson's cat was called Hodge and was much loved by the great man who was not above going out himself to buy oysters for its meals, rather than ask a servant to carry out the task.

Foss was the name of a cat belonging to Edward Lear, the Victorian artist and writer of limericks. Foss featured in many of his rhymes and sketches. Lear had a villa in San Remo, where the cat was his constant companion. When a new hotel development spoiled the view of the sea the poet decided to build another home for himself, but kept strictly to the same design of the original house lest the cat should be displeased by any differences. Lear had problems in human relationships and it has been supposed that the cat was a comfort to him and helped to ease many disappointments. What untold emotions went into the writing of the immortal *The Owl and the Pussy Cat?*

Alexandre Dumas' cat, Mysouff, would walk with him part of the way to his office in the rue St Honoré in Paris, and was to be found waiting at the same place each evening for its master's return.

A great lover of cats was Colette, and she wrote a book called *La Chatte* in which she immortalised her own cat. The creature was called Chatte, as if she were the only cat in the world, and Colette said that she and her husband did not choose her but that *she* chose *them*.

Dickens put many cats into his stories and owned one which was called William – until it produced a litter of kittens! After that, it was known as Williamina. The whole feline family installed itself in the writer's study, somewhat against his will; but when a cat is determined on a course of action, there is little sense in trying to thwart it.

CLASSIC, FABLED AND FAIRY TALE CATS

MRS FORRESTER'S LACE

In Mrs Gaskell's *Cranford*, a Mrs Forrester has her lace collar very much admired by Lady Glenmire during the course of an elegant tea party, upon which she relates the story of her cat:

'Yes, such lace cannot be got now for either love or money . . . I always wash it myself. And once it had a narrow escape . . . Such lace must never be starched or ironed . . . I myself have a very good receipt for washing it in milk . . . Well, ma'am, I had tacked it together (and the beauty of this fine lace is that when it is wet it goes into a very little space) and put it to soak in milk, when unfortunately I left the room; on my return I found pussy on the table looking very like a thief, but gulping very uncomfortably . . . I looked and saw the cup of milk empty – cleaned out . . . ! I was provoked enough to give her a slap, which did no good but only helped the lace down. . . . Then a thought struck me; and I rang the bell for my maid and sent her to Mr Hoggins with my compliments and would he be kind enough to lend me one of his top-boots for an hour? . . . When it came , Jenny and I put pussy in with her fore-feet straight down, so that they were fastened and could not scratch, and we gave her a teaspoonful of currant jelly in which (your ladyship must excuse me) I had mixed some tartar emetic. I shall never forget how anxious I was for the next half-hour. I took pussy to my own room and spread a clean towel on the floor. I could have have kissed her when she returned the lace to sight, very much as it had gone down. Jenny had boiling water ready and we soaked it and soaked it, and spread it on a lavender bush in the sun before I could touch it again . . . But now your ladyship would never guess that it had been in pussy's inside.'

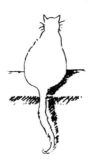

THE CAT THAT WALKED BY ITSELF

Kipling's story of the 'wildest of all the wild animals' (*Felis sylvestris*), who walked by himself and to whom all places were alike, has the classic form of fable with everything parcelled into threes. It deals with the taming of wild Man by the Woman and the further taming by magic of the wild animals in the Wet Wild Woods. The cat watches the dog, horse and cow becoming tamed, but himself makes three stipulations before agreeing to live in the cave to catch mice and amuse the new baby: he demands to come into the cave, to sit by the fire, and to have warm milk three times a day. The Man, however, tougher than the Woman, states his intention of throwing things at the Cat if it does not keep to his side of the bargain.

Kipling points out that, ever since, 'three proper Men out of five will always throw things at a Cat.' One gets the impression that this was not the author's favourite animal.

DICK WHITTINGTON

Dick Whittington's 'cat', some say, was not an animal at all but instead a boat in which he transported coal from Newcastle to London. The story would undoubtedly be of much less interest in the nursery if this belief had become the common interpretation!

PUSS IN BOOTS

This is one of the best-known stories about a magical cat who, through its cunning, brought fame and fortune to its poor master. It appears in various forms in the folk culture of many other countries, although the magical animal is not always a cat.

CATS IN VERSE AND MAXIM
THE FAT CAT SAT ON THE MAT

This phrase used to be the first one used in teaching little children to read, very likely chosen because of its reference to the cherished animal as well as for its useful spelling. Cats were always loved in the nursery, and many rhymes go to prove this:

> As I was going to St Ives,
> I met a man with seven wives,
> Each wife had seven sacks,
> Each sack had seven cats,
> Each cat had seven kits;
> Kits, cats, sacks, and wives,
> How many were going to St Ives?
>
> (Answer: One)

Harley MS. 7316   *c.* 1730

> Ding, dong, bell,
> Pussy's in the well.
> Who put her in?
> Little Johnny Green.
> Who pulled her out?
> Little Tommy Stout.
> What a naughty boy was that
> To try to drown poor pussy cat,
> Who never did him any harm,
> And killed the mice in his father's barn.

Only True Mother Goose Melodies   *c.* 1765

I like little Pussy, her coat is so warm,
And if I don't hurt her, she'll do me no harm.
So I'll not pull her tail, nor drive her away,
But Pussy and I very gently will play.

ibid.   c.1843

Who's that ringing at my door-bell?
I'm a little pussy-cat and I'm not very well.
Then rub your little nose with a little mutton fat,
And that's the best thing for a sick pussy-cat.

Nursery Nonsense and Rhymes,
D'Arcy Wentworth Thompson

The Owl and the Pussy-cat went to sea
In a beautiful pea-green boat.
They took some honey and plenty of money,
Wrapped up in a five-pound note.
The Owl looked up to the stars above,
And sang to a small guitar,
'O lovely Pussy! O Pussy my love,
What a beautiful Pussy you are,
    You are
    You are!
What a beautiful Pussy you are!'

Edward Lear (1812–88)

If I lost my little cat, I should be sad without it.
I should ask St Jerome what to do about it.
I should ask St Jerome, just because of that
He's the only Saint I know that kept a pussy-cat.

Child's poem

'Of all God's creatures, there is only one that
cannot be made slave of the lash. That one is the cat.
If man could be crossed with the cat it would improve
man, but it would deteriorate the cat.'

from Mark Twain's notebook

A London borough displays street signs that advise:
                    DRIVE SAFELY – THINK CAT
                    Concentrate
                    Anticipate
                    Tolerate

ARTISTIC CATS
IN MUSIC AND DANCE

Balanchine created a ballet called *La Chatte* to music by Henri Sauguet for the dancer Olga Spessivtzeva who first danced the feline role in Monte Carlo on 30th April 1927. In 1948, Dame Margot Fonteyn was the woman turned into a cat in Roland Petit's *Les Demoiselles de la Nuit*.

Rossini's cat duet *Duetto Buffo di Due Gatti*, which consists of repeated miaows, is always guaranteed to bring the house down. Another famous cat song features in Ravel's *L'Enfant et les Sortilèges*, an opera about a naughty child who is taught a lesson by the ghosts of animals and objects. The text was written by Colette, who was herself a famous cat lover (see page 30). In the duet for a male and female cat there are only two words, 'minhou' and 'mornao', which are set to exact notes and marked 'nasal'.

More recently, we have Andrew Lloyd Webber's musical show *Cats*, which is peopled with feline characters from T.S. Eliot's *Old Possum's Book of Practical Cats*.

IN ART AND SCULPTURE

Painters have used cats in their work, with Renoir outstanding in portraying the sensual attraction of these animals for humans. Leonardo da Vinci's drawing of a Virgin and Child shows the child on the lap of his mother while he holds a large cat in his arms. The cat seems not to appreciate the honour and is straining to escape.

A delightful work by Goya in 1788 now hangs in the Metropolitan Museum of Art in New York, depicting a little boy in a coral-hued suit sashed in gold who holds a magpie on a lead while three cats stare with obvious intent to pounce. The title is *Don Manuel Osorio de Zuniga with his Cats*.

One has only to visit a museum such as the Fitzwilliam in Cambridge or the British Museum in London to find examples of cats fashioned in a variety of materials, such as Lambeth Delft and agate ware. Fabergé used bowenite to make a very intelligent-looking cat, and the Chinese used cloisonné in the sixteenth century.

PERFORMING CATS

It is possible to train cats to perform but they are not as obedient as dogs or horses. They will jump over a stick or sit up to beg – if in a good humour.

Many years ago, a certain Herr Techow used to exhibit cats who walked on their front legs and jumped through flaming paper hoops. He chose one-year-old animals, never kittens. Stray cats were the best, but even so it would take three years to train them.

Mr Leoni Clarke also showed performing cats in Edinburgh. They did tightrope walking – provided rats, mice and birds were situated along its length.

The most famous performer of recent years was called Arthur, who became a well-loved personality on the small screen, promoting millions of tins of cat food and appearing in some thirty-five films. He gave Press conferences and a biography was written of him. He was kidnapped twice, and he was also involved in a High Court action to determine his rightful owner. The judge, in proper spirit, addressed Arthur with grave courtesy and awarded Spillers custody. His trick of using his left paw to get food out of a tin endeared him to a vast audience; his death, in March 1976 aged nearly seventeen years, caused much mourning among his many fans.

CAT FACTS

SENSES

'When the cat winketh
Little wots the mouse
What the cat thinketh.'
                                    Anon.

SIGHT

Cats' eyes are large in comparison with their skull size and are very sensitive. Each eye can see through an angle of almost 205°, with the help of a most flexible neck. They are placed forward to give stereoscopic vision – unlike many animals which have their eyes on the sides of the head and so receive separate images. The forward position of the eyes means that the cat is able to judge distance quite accurately, but it does also mean that it is less well-equipped to focus on nearby stationary objects. The ability to distinguish objects close to it is also impaired by the cat's natural colour-blindness; it has only one sixth of the human's colour-recording elements in the eye and sees things more in shades of black and white. That is why a cat will have difficulty locating quickly an object which has landed silently nearby, although it will seldom misjudge a jump.

Cats' pupils contract and dilate throughout the day because they react very strongly to light. In the strongest light at noon they will resemble vertical slits, and in dimmer light the pupils will grow rounder again. The cat, however, manages very well in dim light: the iris opens until the pupil grows to a full circle, thus allowing maximum light to enter. This strikes a triangular area in the upper part of the eye (*tapetum lucidum*) where flat cells act as mirrors reflecting light not absorbed by the eye on its way to the retinal cells. This is why we see a cat's eyes shining in the dark.

Cats have an extra eyelid (nictitating membrane or haw) which closes upwards from the inner corner of the eye. It is not completely opaque and allows some light through even when drawn right across. It is used as an added protection against dazzling light, during fights or when going through prickly undergrowth. It may also be drawn up if the cat is, or has been, particularly unwell, and it does help to clean the eye.

The colour of cats' eyes ranges from yellow to orange, chartreuse green to emerald, and from blue to violet, according to breed and coat colour.

A cat's eyes are windows enabling us to
see into another world.

Irish legend

SMELL

The sense of smell is used in territorial marking. This is done by the male who sprays urine to impregnate boundaries and landmarks on his patch with his own odour. A following cat will smell this to determine its age; if it has been deposited for some time and is old, he will proceed to enter this new territory. But if it is fresh, he will usually turn aside in order to avoid an unpleasant encounter. Scent-marking signals the fact that the depositor will probably attack if disturbed.

When a cat, male or female, rubs its head against furniture or a human hand, it is also making a similar territorial mark as there are scent glands on the side of the head.

All cats love the plant called catnip and will roll in borders planted with it. They become even more crazed if they can get at its roots. Some people therefore use the dried leaves to stuff play-balls or toy mice for their pets. However, cats *hate* the smell of rue so much that is used to be the custom to tie sprigs of it under the wings of hens to keep them from being harassed. For the same reason rue used to be fastened to the entrances of dovecotes.

A very clever cat was once known to eat cheese before settling in front of a chosen mousehole. Was it waiting with ba(i)ted breath?!

Touch

Whiskers are for touch sense, but they do not, as one would imagine, represent the width of the body; whiskered animals *do* bump into things. The nose is extremely touch-sensitive, likewise the special long hairs found on the back of the fore-paws which are sensitive to changes in air pressure caused by the presence of obstructions and vibrations. Cats are therefore able to detect and be aware of approaching earthquakes, and imminent storms at sea.

Hearing

When a cat enters a room it will at once find and examine all the sources of sound, such as windows, cracks under doors, grilles, etc. Most humans reach the limit of their hearing with the topmost note of a violin (twenty thousand cycles), but a cat's hearing does not reach its limit until nearly sixty thousand cycles.

Vocalisation

There is a wide range from the 'chirrup' of a mother to her kittens to the full-throated call of a Siamese on heat. 'Miaow' is the sound used in 'talking' to humans and only rarely to another cat. The purr is a sign of pleasure. Snarling and hissing indicate that the cat feels threatened or in danger.

TAILPIECE

The tail of a cat varies in form according to the breed; it may be well-plumed, thick and straight, whip-like, short and full at the base, long and tapered, thin-tipped, round-tipped, with/without kinks. For show purposes the requirements are strictly laid down for every type. Tails may be carried low or erect, and even horizontally over the body as in the case of the White Angora.

Tail movement varies according to the personality of the cat so that the lashing of a tail may not necessarily convey anger or displeasure. Guilt may be shown by a drooping tail, or it may be a sign that the behaviour of humans is causing sheer boredom! Some people claim that when their cat's tail turns over at the tip, it is a form of smile indicating that the animal is feeling pleased. When a cat sits up straight with front paws neatly placed together and then deliberately arranges its tail in a close curve to the front, it seems to say: 'Now I'm ready to listen to you – *if* you have anything sensible to say!'

A cat's tail helps it to keep its balance when walking along narrow ledges, rather like the pole that is carried by tightrope walkers.

Never allow children to pull a cat by its tail. This causes great pain and may provoke some equally painful form of retribution in response.

DEXTERITY

Puss has the ability to jump blind on to a high surface, such as a tabletop, that he cannot see until actually landing on it. However cluttered this may be, he will *usually* manage to avoid all the objects and land neatly among them, presumably due to his stereoscopic vision which can record the layout of the approaching surface in the split second before landing.

DEFENDER AND AGGRESSOR

Confrontation will take place when territorial boundaries have been breached. Cats will give plenty of warning before attacking and will attempt to divert an affray by first engaging in psychological warfare, with displays of strength both threatening and defensive. Hopefully, one of the contenders will thereby give way without too much loss of dignity and with no blood shed!

Glaring, with dilated eyes, open mouth, laid-back ears, bristling fur and tail are defensive signals; stiff legs and raised tails are signals of attack. When the rear quarters advance and the fore parts retreat, forcing the back to arch, this is a mixture of defensive and aggressive signals. Hissing and spitting are warnings intended to shock the enemy and to afford a chance of escape in the resulting confusion. It is the ginger toms who have earned the reputation of being the most aggressive fighters.

CAT CARE

KITTENS

Kittens are usually easy to acquire. It is, perhaps, worth considering contacting your local RSPCA or looking through the local newspaper classified ads before visiting the petshop. Kittens should be at least six weeks old before leaving the mother so that they can feed themselves and quickly be housetrained. Housetraining presents no great difficulty these days with the advent of cat-litter trays, which most kittens readily respond to with very little prompting.

When bringing home a new pet kitten, it is a good idea to place a warm hot-water bottle under a blanket in the box or basket you have prepared for it. This will act as a substitute for its mother's warmth. Some cat-lovers believe that a ticking clock nearby will remind the kitten of its mother's heartbeat. Do avoid draughts; get down on your hands and knees if necessary to test that the bed is free from them.

When the kitten begins to wash itself, this is a sign that it is deciding to stay. An old-fashioned way of helping a cat to settle in a new home is to rub its front paws with butter, which it will lick and, in so doing, start to relax.

Orphaned kittens may be reared by hand with a special feeding bottle or, failing that, an eyedropper or an artist's small paintbrush. *Do not feed with ordinary cows' milk,* which gives kittens diarrhoea. One part boiling water to three parts evaporated milk with a little glucose is recommended.

On a more general note, it is wiser not to watch a cat having her first litter – she will probably be nervous enough as it is – but do let her know that you are at hand if needed and give her praise and a congratulatory stroke afterwards.

49

GROOMING

Grooming consists of combing, brushing, bathing, dry-shampooing and 'polishing'. Combs that are used for different breeds range from fine-toothed to wide, and brushes should be made with natural bristles as man-made ones build up too much static electricity. There are special powders for dry-shampooing to remove dirt and grease, but bran may be used instead on short-haired cats and baby talc on white-haired ones. A final 'polishing' (rubbing in one direction) with a silk cloth or chamois leather imparts a good sheen – an effect that can also be achieved by plenty of hand stroking.

Long-haired cats must have a daily grooming to remove burrs and dead hairs, and to prevent knots and fur balls from forming. This should start with the use of a wide-toothed comb and then a fine one, before going on to a good brushing. Pay special attention to the tufts between the toes. Short-haired cats with very dense, sleek coats will need an equal amount of grooming, but others less well-endowed require only twice-weekly attention.

Eyes, particularly of Persians, must be inspected and any mucus at the corners washed away. Check also that mites are not present in the ears; if they do appear, clean the outer part of the ear very carefully with a cotton bud.

Picking Up Cats

If a cat trusts you it can be picked up in any way. The most comfortable way for the cat, however, is by the forequarters, with some support at the aft end. A mother cat will lift kittens by the scruff, but if a human uses this method on a grown cat, support at the back is needed as soon as the lift starts.

To get a reticent cat out of a corner, aim to scoop it from its back end. A trusting cat that is temporarily being awkward can be grasped by any leg that is within easy reach.

Picking up cats at a height, from a tree for example, should be done from above and, when possible, by the forequarters. Cats get very frightened if there is nothing below them, so make sure to comfort the victim before starting a very slow descent.

Claw Care

It is worth trying to divert a pet cat from clawing at the best upholstery by providing a personal scratching post for the sharpening of claws. A simple version can be made by glue-ing a piece of old carpet to a wooden post which is then nailed to a fixed base. One has, of course, to be prepared for superior cats to ignore such a facility.

Cats insist on an ordered routine in the household and will demonstrate impatience if there is slackness. One red Persian, for example, used to sit on its master's chest first thing in the morning, waiting for him to wake up. If there was any delay in this happening, Tibby would, ever so gently, insert a claw beneath one of his eyelids and prise it open – not a hint to be ignored!

FIRST AID FOR CATS

Cats may take time to learn the dangers of heat, particularly as they love to sit close to its source. They should be trained never to jump on to stove tops or boilers as they have no means of knowing whether they are hot or cold. Burnt paw pads may be smeared with vaseline and wrapped in soft cloth, but not firmly bandaged.

Scalds must be treated by a vet.

Thorns or splinters of wood and glass in the paws should be removed as one would from human flesh. Someone needs to hold the animal fast while the splinter is being removed. Infected wounds need a vet's attention.

Sometimes a cat will play with a length of cotton which is threaded through a needle. If the needle should inadvertently become lodged in the mouth, hold the jaws open as if giving a pill (applying pressure with finger and thumb at the angle of jaw), and grip the needle with tweezers. Again, call on the vet's expertise if you cannot easily deal with the problem. Trapped fish bones and chicken-bone splinters can be dealt with similarly, but such traumas are best avoided by being careful about what is fed to your pet in the first place . . .

If a cat swallows a length of string it will pass safely through. However, if a section starts to trail from its anus, this should be cut short so that the cat cannot attack it. It should on no account be tugged at.

When a cat goes out into the garden and eats grass it is showing good commonsense, for grass is a natural emetic that will enable the cat to bring up any hair that has been swallowed. The variety best liked is called cocksfoot.

Poison, when swallowed, means calling for a vet – fast. If there has to be a delay, get what is named 'the universal antidote', which a chemist will make up. It consists of magnesium oxide, charcoal and tannic acid and it has the ability to absorb many times its own weight of coal-tar poison and strychnine. The dose is one to two tablespoons for a kitten and double the amount for a grown cat. In an emergency, a home-made version of milk of magnesia, burnt toast, and strong tea may be administered.

Do not try to remove wet paint on the fur with turpentine, but wipe the area affected with a dry cloth and clip the fur where necessary.

CATS ON HOLIDAY

It is especially important to remember that a cat must have free access to a supply of water at all times as it is essential for its general diet and well-being. It should also be remembered that cats are *not* self-sufficient by nature and should therefore have proper provision made for their care when their owners go away. Leaving a cat on its own in the house with cans of opened cat food is not the answer! Call on a friend or neighbour to perform the daily feeding routine and to maintain some sort of contact with the 'abandoned' animal.

It is also becoming more acceptable for certain pets to accompany their owners to holiday destinations, so if your cat is a good traveller – and Siamese cats, for example, tend actually to *enjoy* a car journey – then a holiday away may not necessarily mean parting from your cat.

When moving to a new house it is a wise precaution to shut your cat into a room for a couple of days so that it becomes familiar with it and thinks of it as 'home'. If this is not done, the cat is unlikely to return to its new, unfamiliar surroundings once let out to wander.

As a rule, cats venture forth in ever increasing circles around their home centres.

CATS AND THE LAW

The law in Britain says that when a dog is involved in a road accident the incident must be reported to the police, but the same does not apply for a cat. The reasoning behind this is that a cat is classified as a wild animal. Neither is a cat-owner responsible for misdeeds perpetrated by their animal, even if it kills a neighbour's pet canary. On the other hand, compensation *is* due to the owner of a cat if a person deliberately inflicts cruelty upon it. Cats are not taxed in Britain but they do come under the protection of the Acts that protect all animals from abandonment and cruelty. Fines and imprisonments can ensue if someone is found guilty of such crimes.

In the United States and many other parts of the world the cat is protected to some extent, but it may be required to wear a bell around its neck. It may also run the risk of being humanely destroyed if found killing birds.

In rented accommodation it is often forbidden to keep pets, but there are, as may be imagined, many feline tenants who live an undercover life while official blind eyes are turned. However, one lady in a sheltered home, who brought two cats with her when she moved in, threatened to jump from the balcony if anyone from the estate office tried to evict them. Needless to say, clemency prevailed and all three were permitted to continue to live together unharassed.

COMMON CAT BREEDS

EUROPEAN TABBY

This is the most widespread domestic cat, being adaptable and friendly as a pet. It has a long body with short hair and a standard pattern of markings. These consist of three dark stripes along the spine, ending at the tail. The chest is barred with two horizontal stripes and often a third one at the base of the neck. There are oval patches on the shoulders joining those on head and paws, giving a butterfly pattern that can be seen from above when a tabby squats. An oyster pattern appears on the flanks. The head has markings which converge on the nose and form the M-mark attributed to the love that Mohammed felt towards cats (see page 12).

There are three basic colours among tabbies: red, silver, and brown, which is the most common. Most of the short-haired cats we have as pets today are the offspring of tabby cats, regardless of colour and markings.

The word 'tabby' derives from a taffeta or ribbed silk which, when calendered or watered, becomes covered in wavy lines. This pattern used to be called 'tabby' and was therefore used to describe the markings on this cat's fur.

LONG-HAIRED CATS

These were unknown in Europe until the end of the sixteenth century, and it was not until the time of the Crystal Palace Cat Show of 1871, when pedigree records began to be kept and breeding had begun, that they were seen in numbers. The Persian type was preferred to the Turkish Angora (named after the city of Angora, now Ankara), and soon the title of 'Persian' became applicable to all long-haired domestic cats.

PERSIAN

A true Persian has a 'cobby' (short and thick) body, low with short, thick legs. The tail is bushy and carried low, and the fur silky, never woolly, with a ruff around the head which continues as a jabot down between the front legs. There are long tufts on the ear tips and a bushy tip to the tail. Cheeks are broad, the nose is snub with with a marked break known as a 'stop' where it joins the skull. Ears are well-spaced, small and set low.

White Persians with blue eyes are generally deaf and are therefore particularly vulnerable to the dangers of road traffic. They are often said to be poor mothers as they are unable to hear the cries of their kittens.

TURKISH

The breed now known by this title arrived in Europe as late as 1955, when a pair was brought over by an English breeder. They were first known as Van Cats because they came from the area of the lake of that name in south-east Turkey. Official recognition of these cats was only granted in 1969. This animal is chalky white with auburn markings on the face and tail. It has an unusual liking for water and appears to swim for pleasure, unlike most cats who only do so in an emergency.

A full list of long-haired cats is very extensive and includes many different colourings. Such a list would include: brown, blue, silver, red, and cream tabbies; chinchilla, shaded silver, and tortoiseshell cameos; black, cream, black smoke, and parti-coloured Persians; seal, chocolate point, and lilac Himalayan: seal point, and blue point Balinese; chocolate point Birman; Somali, and even the Cymric, which is a long-haired type of Manx cat.

SIAMESE

These cats existed for two hundred years in Siam before the first pair came to England, probably as a gift from the King to the British Consul. They were shown at the Crystal Palace in 1885. They had rounder faces and darker coats than those of today, and they also had a kinked tail and squinting eyes, which have mostly been bred out by now.

The two main types of Siamese are the Seal Point and Blue Point. The Seal Point has a dark brown face, ears, paws and tail, with the body fur a fawny-brown on top, shading to cream underneath. The Blue Point has the same markings but the dark patches are blue and the body fur silvery beige. New-born kittens are almost white, but the markings generally appear during the course of the first year.

The Siamese head has a pointed outline with ears broad set and wide open at their base, which gives the cat an alert expression. The back legs are slightly longer than the fore legs so that the animal perpetually appears as if it is about to spring. They are prolific breeders. The kittens need to be left with the mother until they are at least twelve weeks old.

The range of colour in Siamese cats includes chocolate point, lilac point, and red point, as well as tortie points and tabby points of different shades. They have vivid blue eyes and are very vocal, especially if they are left on their own! They need plenty of companionship.

BURMESE

The breed as we know it today was only developed in 1930 in the United States, when a cat of oriental type was imported from Burma. There being no similar cat to mate it with, a Siamese was chosen. The resulting breed was popular on account of its intelligent, affectionate personality and quieter voice, together with a nature less destructive than that of the pure Siamese. These cats were imported into the United Kingdom in 1948. When the Blue first appeared however, it was so unexpected that it was named Sealcoat Blue Surprise. The eyes of a Burmese are a deep or golden yellow, and their fur colouring overall predominantly bluish-grey, though shading paler on the underparts. A Burmese cat loves people, is very good with children, and hates to be left alone.

Rex

This cat is an unusual one with a short, curly coat that may be of any colour. The first cat known to have had this kind of coat was born in Germany in the 1940s. This creature's kittens were later transported to the United States, where another strain developed. There are also two English strains: the Cornish and the Devon, which first appeared in those counties in 1950 and 1960 respectively.

The Rex was first recognised as a breed in 1967 and is now accepted all over the world. The Cornish type is slender, muscular and hard, and stands with an arched back on long straight legs. The Devon Rex has the same build, a coarser coat, and really huge ears. Both types love people, have a sense of fun, and will tolerate a harness or a lead more readily than other types of domestic cat. They are, however, also hearty eaters and should be prevented from becoming obese.

Manx

Tail-less cats have appeared in various parts of the world but the term 'Manx' (meaning Isle of Man) is significant as an island home ensures a completely insular breeding ground. This has perpetuated a characteristic that would otherwise have been naturally bred out, being a seemingly unnatural trait.

For competition purposes a Manx must display a complete absence of tail and have a hollow at the site where it would have begun. This cat has a short backbone and well-developed hindquarters. The hind legs are longer than the fore legs, which gives it a hopping gait, (thus giving rise to the

legend that the Manx cat is the result of a cross between a rabbit and a cat). Its coat can be of any colour. It is a good friend to man and makes an efficient ratter.

A scholarly barrister was recently found scratching with a penknife a Latin epitaph on the gravestone of his beloved cat, Waffles. In a voice hoarse with emotion he read out and translated the lines, then sternly reminded the listener of the fact that *dignus* takes the ablative!

> *'Dormitat hic felis quo non mortalibus*
> *ullus gratior. Heus! gremio dignior*
> *ille Jovis.'*

Roughly translated:

> 'Here good old Waffles takes a nap.
> He'll soon be sitting on God's lap.'